SARGON BOULUS

Sargon Boulus (1944–2007) remains one of the best-known and most influential of contemporary Arab poets. Born into an Assyrian Iraqi family, and growing up in Al-Habbaniyah, Kirkuk and Baghdad, he started publishing his own work in 1961 in the ground-breaking *Shi'r [Poetry]* magazine in Beirut. After settling in San Francisco in the late 1960s, he became an unstoppable translator of English-language modern poets into Arabic and dedicated his life to reading, writing and translating poetry, every so often making forays to Europe to meet up with fellow exiles and perform at festivals. His untimely death, in Berlin in October 2007 at the aged of 63, left "a gaping wound in the heart of modern Arabic poetry".

He has six poetry collections of his own work and has translated numerous British and American poets into Arabic. He has two bilingual collections in Arabic and German, one of poetry and one of short stories, he also co-authored *Legenden und Staub*, with Bosnian author Safeta Obhodjas (2002). He was a contributing editor, and later a consulting editor, for *Banipal* from its first issue in February 1998.

Sargon Boulus played an invaluable role in introducing to Arab poets and readers major modern English-language poets, including Ezra Pound, W. H. Auden, W. S. Merwin, Ted Hughes, William Carlos Williams, Allen Ginsberg, Gary Snyder, Sylvia Plath, Robert Duncan, John Ashbury, Robert Bly, Anne Sexton, John Logan and Michael Ondaatje, as well as other poets such as Rilke, Neruda, Vasko Popa and Ho Chi Min.

Sargon started assembling this collection, *Knife Sharpener*, whose title he chose, in the months before he died. It is published now, in an extended form, as a posthumous commemoration and celebration of Sargon Boulus, bringing together for the first time all the poems, written between 1991 and 2007, that he translated himself, together with an essay, "Poetry and Memory", written especially for this volume.

SARGON BOULUS

Knife Sharpener

Selected Poems

translated from the Arabic
by the author

Banipal Books
2009

First published in the UK by Banipal Books, London 2009

Copyright © 2007 Sargon Boulus
Translation copyright © 2009 Banipal Publishing
Introduction copyright © 2008 Pat Boran.
All photograpahs © Banipal Publishing

The poems in this collection were translated from
the original Arabic by the author
from his collections *Hamil al-Fanous fi Lail el-Dhi'ab* (1996),
Idha Kunta Na'iman fi Markabi Nooh (1998), and *Al-Awal
wal-Tali* (2000) and from unpublished poems

A CIP record for this book is available in the British Library
ISBN 978-0-9549666-7-6

Banipal Books
1 Gough Square, LONDON EC4A 3DE, UK
www.banipal.co.uk/banipalbooks/

Set in Bembo
Printed and bound in the UK

Sargon Boulus
1944–2007

In commemoration and celebration

CONTENTS

Knife Sharpener

Sargon Boulus at James Joyce's statute, Dublin

HIGH AND VERTICAL

As it is, not as metre or rhyme. This is how Sargon
Boulus views poetic writing and how he practises it.
Writing, for him, is another existence within exis-
tence. Thus he only encounters himself as he encoun-
ters the world. When he avoids, moves away, and
secludes himself, it is for one purpose: to complete the
distance required for this encounter which allows him
to see well and to know how to penetrate and look
ahead.

He does not engage in polemics. Let what is good be
good for its people. And let what is evil be evil for its
people. Let those who want to clash, clash. He prefers
to stay in the light. In the navel of the thing, high and
vertical. Values are swings and light is beyond all direc-
tions. What is "the message"?

Water seeps through and goes deep.
The air touches the rose and the thorn with the same
    hand.
The wing is the closest sibling to the horizon.
There is no separation between reality and what is
    beyond it:

Imagination, for Sargon Boulus, is mixed, kneaded
  with material as if it is another body in his body.
Sargon's poetry asks me.
And that is why I love him.

Adonis
Paris, 20 October 2007

Adonis wrote this Foreword to *Knife Sharpener*
just two days before Sargon Boulus died

INTRODUCTION

There are not many people one can truly call a poet –
in the sense of an individual whose entire life seems
dedicated to, even composed by, poetry: but Sargon
Boulus was one of them. Like a lot of people, from the
moment I first met Sargon, at the Dublin Writers Fes-
tival in 2003 for a celebration of contemporary Arab
writing, I felt I was in the presence of someone truly
significant. For here was a poet who was clearly deeply
wounded by the recent events in his homeland of Iraq,
but not just those recent events: like all great poets Sar-
gon seemed to feel also the even greater, historical
weight of conflicts, tensions, misunderstandings and
oppressions of the spirit, as if his poems came through
his own time and language but from somewhere else.
No doubt this was in part due to the fact that he wrote
in Arabic, a language which offered (if not demanded)
historical coherence and continuity in ways I could
only imagine.

The audience at that Dublin Writers Festival event
was, no doubt like myself, expecting a certain amount
of political observation. This was in mid June: three
months earlier the US and its allies had commenced
"the liberation of Iraq". And yet what we heard from
Boulus and his fellow writers – Samuel Shimon, Has-
souna Mosbahi and Maram Al-Massri, introduced by

Banipal's Margaret Obank – was in general that much longer view of history, that much longer view of the writer's role in the world. This seemed particularly the case with Sargon.

W B Yeats's notion about the relationship between poetry and politics has seldom seen clearer expression than in the poetry of Sargon Boulus: "We make out of the quarrel with others, rhetoric, but of the quarrel with ourselves, poetry," wrote Yeats, apparently presenting an either/or choice that has caused many a poet to stumble. Not a political poet, certainly not trusting of the unexamined impulse to make political verse, nevertheless in the words of Saadi Youssef, Sargon Boulus "stood against the occupation of Iraq because poets must be against occupation".

Of course Boulus could never have been a political poet, even if that had been his goal. For, as he says himself in this volume, "when I write, I am actually remembering, not the past itself, not a person or a place, a scene or sound or song, but first and foremost I am remembering words". This withdrawal from agreed, shared, external experience into the zone of the imagination is unlikely to go well with any purely political movement; but it is also interesting to note that Sargon's approach to poetry is not directed exclusively to self, is not simply a diary in verse of the poet's inner life. By nailing his colours to words – the building blocks of experience – he avoids the either/or dichotomy confronted by Yeats and finds not a middle but a third way, a path whose ground seems sometimes both, sometimes neither but on which the poet cannot fail to tread. As some of the best of Neruda's "political" poetry came from his realization that the world of objects carried the history of those who made them ("The contact these objects have had with man and earth may serve as a valuable lesson to a tortured lyric poet"), so too does Sargon find a meaningful connection between the lyric and personal and the wider historical imperatives. As he says himself, "I believe that any given language contains all the memory traces of the communities that contributed to it. For a poet, nothing is lost."

And the poet who lives during wartime and is "beseiged by the cries / of his tribe as he wanders / among the bones / and walks through the ruins / of his city", what is there for him to do? He can only dream

> of flying like an eagle
> over the heads of the slain
> and their slayers,
> hoping to catch a fabulous
> creature swift in its flight
> with his words,
> and to plant the hook
> of his imagination
> into the flesh of his prey.

Even so, "What the words / can do, / is almost nothing / in these days" as he says in "The Mystery of Words" suggesting perhaps not that words are meaningless or powerless (otherwise why devote one's life to them) but that "in these days" they can only fail; for words enact their magic slowly, demand of us a wider, longer view of our time on this earth, our place in things.

Sargon Boulus's poems are full of death, and violence, and darkness, but they are also very much concerned with life and birth. Indeed birth features many times and in many ways in these poems, in the sense of the poet as a kind of midwife, certainly, but also in the real joy and hope of new arrival: the beautiful image of "a face / shining under the rags / in its tiny cradle / luminous like a loaf of bread" in the poem "The Legend of Al-Sayyab and the Silt" or the no less miraculous but considerably more urgent deliveries performed by Umm Youssef, the apparently beloved midwife who pulls babies "out of the warm darkness of the womb / into the starkness of this world / by her dextrous hands".

★ ★ ★

There is a timeless quality about the best of this work, as there must be to the work of a poet who will be remembered. Opening with a verse that sees the poet waiting for a wave "that will cast me / onto an unknown /shore, tied / to a stone" ("How Oriental Singing was Born"), the poems set out hoping for salvation in suffering but expecting, and finding, suffering in salvation: this they know is the two-edged sword of art which teaches us "how to sing / with this wounded / voice".

Consolation, but less frequently, escape from suffering most often comes from nature, from a necessary synchronization of the self to the rhythms and processes of the natural world. The poem "Butterfly Dream", for instance, balances an image of the poet "shaking last night's / nightmares / from my head" with the image of a passing butterfly gliding over the garden fence, a butterfly "that only yesterday / was a mere caterpillar, / trapped in its narrow cocoon". Again there is an opportunity, or demand, for a second take here, as it is not the poet who is compared to the butterfly but the poet's nightmares (trapped in his head) which are compared to the butterfly, said to be "like a tiny prayer or dream". What might at first be taken for a fairly conventional simile (haunted, earth-bound poet and recently freed caterpillar) might in fact be more about the content of vision, of imagination, the necessity of giving expression to nightmare as well as dream, dark thoughts in bright times as well as vice versa. For just as the butterfly flies free, the poet is "shaking last night's / nightmares / from my head", as if the nightmares too, like the caterpillar, might be released from their cocoon and given their darker freedom.

★ ★ ★

For someone born in a desert (and who walked across the desert from Baghdad to Beirut), it is hardly surprising that desert should feature so prominently in Sargon's writing: "The desert stretches in my dreams, rife with / promises, with dangers, with cautionary tales" ("This Road Alone"). In the poem "The Borders" a village that once had water flowing through its orchards is "nothing but a river of sand now, / gluttonous with the force of oblivion". The desert is all-consuming. Out of it may have come so much of what makes up our varied civilizations, but in it lurks the death of those very civilizations, as if following in their footsteps.

But perhaps even more than desert one encounters the presence of a terrible wind throughout these poems, a wind that "comes down / to bleed like a mother, and scream / and give birth" ("Legacy with a Taste of Dust"); a wind that may at once "blow savage from the direction / of slaughter, hot like / the breath of a furnace" ("A Song for the One who will Walk to the End of the Century") or later may simply lift the skirts of a woman in a graveyard: either way there is always the threat that this wind may eventually remove all trace of people "as if they never walked the earth"

("News About No One").

There is an extraordinary poem, "Incident in a Mountain Village" in which a rock tumbles from a mountain-side, disturbing all the birds in the area, as it finally lodges itself "into the mouth / of the well". What are we to make of this uncanny moment, the seeming precision of the force which brings the rock to its resting place, blocking up the source of life (civilization) itself. Here, arguably, is war and conflict but again with an almost Yeatsian flavour. One cannot help but notice, too, that it is a mouth that is stuffed, silenced, in the closing lines, making this 'natural' occurrence almost an act of punishment.

A more literal kind of punishment and, by extension, witnessing, features in "A Boy Against the Wall" in which a boy hides his eyes behind the leaves of a blueberry branch, unable to endure the stares of neighbours "leaning over the walls / like a gathering of crows" to watch his father being publicly flogged. Perhaps it is fortuitous that the English noun for "a gathering of crows" is "murder"; if so, it illustrates how Sargon's belief that words have a life of their own is evidently true. It is also, of course, further reminder that if the story can come to us from anywhere, then we too are often unable to perceive it, that just like the place of massacre which the blind man in "Witness" unknowingly walks through, the things closest to us might also be said to have "vanished into the distance".

Witnessing, in a time of war, inevitably involves mourning, and a strong emotional constitution. To avoid being turned to stone (a word with often negative connotations in the work of Sargon Boulus) is perhaps the greatest challenge for those who survive: to acknowledge if hardly accept the statement, "for us, / always the mourning, / for you always / the victory / parade" ("Widow Maker, Mother of Woes").

★ ★ ★

That words have independent existences is, of course, a fact which daily confronts the would-be translator; even so, Boulus gave so much of his time and energy to the translation of a wide range of writing (and of course to the translation of his own work, always written in Arabic and then sometimes carried across to an English language readership).

In a complex poem like "In the Midst of Giving Birth", conflict goes on even as poems are created, or struggle to come into being. What goes on outside the door of the poem threatens "the flesh of words", and the world outside: "I see the killer fire his gun; / the poem crumbles in my hands". And yet Sargon manages to make a poem that is about so much more than just the act of writing.

Perhaps politics is not, as we sometimes imagine, separate to daily living. Even so there are times when

Sargon comes close to pointing a finger, as in "This Master Who". "This is / a master who / came / from America / to drink / from the Tigris / and / the Euphrates" – the almost telegraphically shortened lines perhaps suggesting William Carlos Williams (so admired by Sargon) but the tone, the simultaneous restraint and accusation suggesting the almost spell-like power of words so often found in the holy books of the world, another example of the poet's method of reaching in two directions at once.

"The Story Will Be Told" reminds us that it is not important how the sustaining truth finds its way to us, or where it comes from, so long as it comes. "So are the tales spun / from nothing," Sargon writes, embracing, as ever, the mystery. "If the Words Should Live", meanwhile, suggests that for the sake of words "we kill and die, / and are nourished / by their dazzling poverty".

★ ★ ★

As has been noted many times elsewhere, Sargon Boulus was a wanderer, a traveller in both the geographic and temporal senses, engaged in the journey of poetry that can set one down anywhere but seldom convincingly calls any one place home. Where a Californian sunset recalls the pattern and colours of a Persian carpet, almost inevitably the mountain of San

Bruno below it becomes a mountain on which the poet might and perhaps must be lifted into flight: for this mountain topped with radio towers (symbols of communication, after all, of distance made immaterial, traversible) becomes, at the end of the poem, ominously, a place "where the lights / flash red / on the towers, / and stab the sky". No vision even of the natural world is safe from the intrusion of human concerns.

In "Execution of the Falcon", an eerie scene in the Nevada desert sees a man execute his faithful old companion which has lost its "killer instinct", releasing it to soar in the air one last time even as he takes careful aim with his rifle and brings it down in "a tiny plume of dust". The violence here, however, seems understood as necessary. The man picks up the dead falcon "almost tenderly", then tosses it onto his pick-up truck and roars off "into the desert / and the night". Oblivion is inescapable; death like life is ever on the move.

★ ★ ★

"And the earth floats, a vagabond, among the stars." ("This Road Alone")

In this arrangement of Sargon's poems, begun by the poet himself in the months before he died and completed by Margaret Obank, there are heart-stoppingly sad moments as one reaches what seems to be his adieu, his farewell to alms, as it were, to their giving and receiving. "Invocations Before Sailing" ends in a voice that Sargon pretty much perfected, one in which he has just earlier spoken of the detail and the horror of war and death, but which now draws back a little, back to the simple essentials, the basic ingredients of survival for any living creature, us imperfect humans included.

Sargon Boulus was not with us long enough, and though he often talked of a collection of his poems in English, perhaps there was some doubt that it could ever happen, or that, as a traveller in another language, he could ever do more for it than wish it luck, salute and move on. And now that he has moved on, and left many of us the luckier for having known him, I sense in it his warmth, his hurt and his humanity, and ultimately his salute to us in language across the otherwise untranslatable distances.

> Let there be always under your feet
> some generous land to make you feel safe.
> If one day it proves to be
> too narrow, find the sea. And sail.
> (from "Invocations Before Sailing")

Pat Boran
Dublin, October 22, 2008
(the first anniversary of Sargon Boulus's death)

POETRY AND MEMORY

"I am here. Those three words contain all that
can be said – you begin with those words and
you return to them. Here means on this earth,
on this continent, and no other, in this city
and no other, and this epoch I call mine, this
century, this year. I was given no other place,
no other time, and I touch my desk to defend
myself against the feeling that my own body is
transient. This is all very fundamental, but after
all, the science of life depends on the gradual
discovery of fundamental truths."

Czeslaw Milosz

A poet deals with time as it slips through his fingers
drop by drop and evaporates into nothing. "The drop
that doesn't become a river is devoured by the sands,"

says Ghalib★ in one of his ghazals, or love poems. Time after time I make the discovery that, when I write, I am actually remembering, not the past itself, not a person or a place, a scene or sound or song, but first and foremost I am remembering words. Words and their reverberations in memory. The words that reside in a certain memory, that carry the echoes of a certain time and place. But the problem for a poet is not essentially one of vocabulary; the problem is how to take the old vocabulary and put it in new settings, in new structures that will speak of our present and illuminate what is happening now. So the function of memory is not simple: one needs to know the words and what they mean, but one needs also to forget the settings in which they were found.

Willingly or not, I keep going back and forth into the past. Poetry is a great method of mining the hidden areas of what has been lived through, the shadowy regions where endless discoveries lie awaiting you, all that material that has made you what you are; the places where you have lived, the times and circumstances, all the things that have shaped you. So, for me, the process of going back through memory is very important, back into those details that do not exist in anybody's head but mine. Childhood, then, is a magical source that lies between shadow and light, so deeply embedded in the past that it is always possible to evoke it with new shadings that may fall into the realm of dreams.

I was born in a small town called Al-Habbaniyah, in the middle of Al-Dulaim desert, where only the Bedouins and goat herders could survive. That is why the artificial lake around which the town was built had a powerful presence in the lives of the inhabitants, mostly Assyrians who were brought there by the British after their families were massacred and driven out of their homes, first by Ottoman Turks and Kurds in 1915 and then by Iraqi military and Kurds from northern Iraq in 1933. Al-Habbaniyah became a British military air base. My father used to work in the base, like most of the other Assyrians, some of whom were recruited into the Levies, along with Indian Sikhs whose intricately arranged beards and turbans fascinated us no end. One of my very first and cherished memories is of when my father took me to his place of work on this base where only the English lived, surrounded by an enormous fence. This was when I saw English women for the first time, having their tea, seemingly almost half-naked among their flowers and well-kept lawns, some of them covered with freckles like cantaloupes or snakes; a totally different kind of female to our mothers and sisters who were wrapped in black most of the time and looked as if they had just come back from a funeral. It was like sneaking through a hole in the wall of paradise, finding yourself in another world.

Soon we left Al-Habbaniyah and moved to Kirkuk, a

city in the north with almost no water except for a small river that was dry nine months of the year, then suddenly flooded its banks and drowned the sheep and cows and horses, and quite a few people besides. The memory of this phenomenon was so persistent that I couldn't help but express it, almost thirty years later, in the poem "Witnesses on the Shore", which I wrote in San Francisco and which is included in this book. So, from the lush gardens of the tea-drinking English ladies to a city that was dry and rocky-soiled, but redolent of the petrol that flared day and night in the oilfields of the Iraqi Petroleum Company, or IPC, so that people walked by its light in the middle of the night as if it were daytime; quite a Gulliverian trip for a small boy. The oil was everywhere, almost everyone worked for the company (run, of course, by the eternal British). Here, the people were mostly Turkomen, many of whom lived in an ancient citadel wrapped in mystery – it was as if history was there facing you every day. Assyrian, Armenian, Turkoman, Kurdish and Arab history were all intermingled and moulded together like a huge tower of Babel. That is why, when I write my poetry in Arabic, which is seventy per cent Assyrian (Aramaic and Syriac), I feel I am intoning all these voices, for I believe that any given language contains all the memory traces of the communities that contributed to it. For a poet, nothing is lost.

A writer is a witness to his age. It is all a matter of

being aware, in the middle of chaos and madness, war and massacre, of those faint voices that tell us about times gone by, about other lives that are buried in the belly of the whale we call history. Poets live most of their lives waiting for something, a hidden fact that might reveal itself, just because a certain other fact happens to trigger a connection, out of nowhere. Some of them, the lucky ones, the great ones, may sometimes get the whole story in one line, or image, or poem. I was always fascinated, and endlessly puzzled, by this saying of Paul Celan's: "Our talk of justice is empty until the largest battleship has foundered on the forehead of a drowned man." Somehow, it says it all: the impossibility of being what we are, and the possibility of becoming what we can be.

It was Gertrude Stein who got it right when she said: "Writers have to have two countries, the one where they belong and the one in which they live really. The second one is romantic, it is separate from themselves, it is not real but it is really there . . . of course sometimes people discover their own country as if it were the other." If there ever was a true definition of exile, it is this. And I mean the eternal exile, without the sentimentality of yearning for return (for, in reality, there is no return: "You can't step into the same river twice.") Once an immigrant, eternally one. "Paradise" can never be regained.

There is a tale attributed to Rumi that says: "A man

went to the door of the beloved and knocked. A voice asked him from inside: 'Who is there?' 'It is me,' the man answered. 'This place is not big enough for you and me, I'm afraid,' said the voice. And the door stayed closed. The man went away, confused and perplexed, wondering about those words, contemplating their hidden meanings. After a year of living in solitude, depriving himself of the simplest pleasures of life, he finally decided to go again and knock on the door. The same voice asked him from inside: 'Who is there?' 'It is you,' the man answered, and the door was opened for him." Of course, to the Sufi, a whole series of rigorous spiritual exercises has to be gone through in order for the door to be opened, so he can enter into the presence of the beloved, as the mystics call God. However, the task of the poet, whose only tools are words, is different. For him the door remains locked until he succeeds, through sheer dedication, in penetrating the mystery of language itself. And because art is long and life is short, according to Horace, no individual poet has ever been able to achieve this formidable task completely, even the greatest ones. What happens is that throughout history each poet, whether consciously or not, continues the work of the poets who came before him, something like an endless poem extending into eternity, or the end of time.

Czeslaw Milosz wrote a poem that said exactly this; it tells of the incredible journey poets of all ages take, usually as a band of human beings who choose their own way, are bent on telling the truth – usually in a quixotic and sometimes childish way, who are shunned by the society at which they rave, always on the side of the weak and the oppressed, praising a flower or the innocence of a child or a woman's beauty. Although poets might stab a rival in the back out of envy, Milosz wrote, they will still translate each other into their own tongue for they know they are together in all this. After all, they are the ones who have made the choice between "the perfection of the life, or the work" as Yeats wrote in his poem "The Choice". In the same vein, Borges, in his essay "Coleridge's Rose", has repeated a similar idea that all poets have been elabo-rating the same ancient epic, of which each poem is

Czeslav Milosz and Sargon Boulus, London, 1998

only a fragment.

I liked Milosz's poem so much that I translated it into Arabic and it was published in an Arab daily newspaper in London, where the Nobel laureate was to give a reading at the London Poetry International Festival. The great poet was fascinated by the shape of the Arabic letters when I showed it to him, and asked me eagerly which poem it was. I told him it was "A Report" and that it was obviously raised to God, or some entity he called "O Most High". Milosz beamed. "Oh, yes of course," he said. "You know, I have sent Him many reports through the years but He has never answered me." I couldn't help saying to the great poet: "Who knows, maybe one day He will." At the time I'm speaking of, Milosz was eighty-seven, but still robust and alert for his age. It was tremendously refreshing, to say the least, to stand in the presence of this great poet. Here was a true witness of the age, a man who had been through war and madness, seen a whole civilization go to ruin and, through sheer love of poetry and the ultimate passion that drives it, survived to tell the tale.

Sargon Boulus
San Francisco, April 2007

★ Ghalib was an important 19th-century Urdu poet, famous for his numerous ghazals, or love poems, which are published in English translation as *Love Sonnets of Ghalib* (2002).

Sargon Boulus, Schöppingen, 2000

HOW ORIENTAL SINGING WAS BORN

Prophet

I gather myself
into one,
exposing my face
to lightning,
and rave
while waiting
for a wave
that will cast me
onto an unknown
shore, tied
to a stone.

Book

Open
the book of time
with trembling
fingers, and read:
your life chained
to this page;
your lover
who will tell you
her first secret

and her last.

God

God decreed
that the underworld
be revealed in
this one:
these dark, sad,
twisted alleys
where men are
condemned
to drift forever.

Oud

Then the days
went rolling by,
and one day
somebody shoved
this oud between
my hands,
and taught me
how to sing
with this wounded
voice.

MEKNES, MOROCCO

For those who
come from far,
Meknes lies
behind its walls
like hot bricks
cooling off in a kiln.

Under the arches
of its domes,
caravans rest
by the gates waiting
for a sign.

A horse without
a saddle stands motionless
in the shade.

Berber women
sell their trinkets, beads,
and flying carpets
by the road.

Day is only
an excuse for arriving
sooner into

the realms of night,
as it is fueled
by the Ramadan moon
for the benefit of those
who fast and sleep
soundly
on the roofs.

Across the few
remaining nights,
the feast will surely
come, when laughter
becomes an extra
dimension
orbiting the circuit
of our grief
and the stork's nest
looks bigger
than the post office.

THE SIEGE

I woke up in this house,
kept by a woman who disappears
for weeks at a time, to wander along the river.
When she comes back, she moors
her light skiff to my thigh
while I sleep, and drags her bruised body
in heavy silence to my bed.

Roaming freely in the alleys,
beasts recently set free grow more
ferocious by the hour, pouncing on children,
mauling the sick, while rumours spread
with the other news: that a great
famine, that the plague,
the daily massacres . . .

When the day arrives, its carts
piled with fresh ammunition, my neighbours
bang their heads against the doors, a sign
of total submission, or unbearable pain.

HE WHO GOES TO THE PLACE

This obstacle, for instance: as though, just healed
from a sickness, you awoke to find a stone under
your head, far from your destination, the point that
flashes then goes off like the eye of a nocturnal
animal wary of the hunter; under a monument, in a
place, a public square with its own hooded crowd,
where you appear, on the verge of embracing
whatever is passing, then you resume your way.

This tomorrow, for instance, that sways like a sword
over the guest's head, as he hurries past the
open gates of hell, carrying on his back an ancient
hand-press, a raving idol, a woman with a frozen
waterfall between her legs that will not flow unless
whipped by the devil himself.

Because you either never answered the letter, or
you never went anywhere. But you arrived at the
place.

THE BORDERS

Where the sun used to dance
on window panes in some village,
on water flowing through the orchards,
there is nothing but a river of sand now,
gluttonous with the force of oblivion,
on whose banks nothing grows but time,
here, on the other side of the border.
Tyre marks stretch in the dunes,
then vanish, only to appear once more
behind the border, between two walls
that scale the sky; a vulture floats
like a forgotten worshipper
in an abandoned temple,
over the head of the man passing
under spans of mirages
anointed by no one, across
a horizontal ladder of dunes;
he flies low to examine a lizard
racing in the shadow of his wings,
the loosened stakes of a tent,
perforated tin cans storing rust,
or the bones of a smuggler, a beast.
Beneath a rag nailed by the thorns
like a banner of defeat,
the coiled serpent sleeps.

The dry artesian well shelters
a few crickets at dusk, the wind
goes aimless on its way,
and the hour is naked, burdened
with the weight of separation.
Here the man turns his back to the vulture.

INCIDENT IN A MOUNTAIN VILLAGE

The air is suddenly
incensed, night shivers

inside the tree,
as we listen to a storm

of fluttering wings
that rise by their thousands

in the dark: it is the birds
fleeing from a rock

that fell headlong
from its height

on the mountain-side,
and lodged itself

into the mouth
of the well.

IN PRAISE OF ENCOUNTERS

We leave a fire
wherever we are,
then long for the sea
in its mighty solitude.
Someone gazes
into the void,
guarded by the idols
of his inner dark.

For there is within
each one of us a shore
to welcome
the oncoming wave.
But this world
that is nothing but a mould
fashioned with all
our bodies, is both
the player and his guitar.

Let me smash these
beautiful records
against the floor of this night
like Easter eggs.
I have heard
enough music to last me

the rest of my days.
Let me dismantle
these wooden shelves
(I no longer need
those books filled
with wisdom).

Let me follow those
flames that race among
the trees, where the wind
dances naked like Salomé,
after winning
on a silver platter
John the Baptist's head.

If I keep feeding the fire,
smoke might lead me
to the place
where I can worship
something beyond you or me,
until it is revealed
to my eyes.

Any shadow can be
my guide, help me
find my words, as I carry
my nets down to the river,
where the living surge

and meet, then go
on their way.

IN THE MIDST OF GIVING BIRTH

Night with its restless stars,
spark-infested, heavy with doom;
those thorns planted
in the flesh of words
are the crown
woven for a woman's head,
she who thrashes
in the pangs of giving birth.

Her piercing shriek
punctures the birth-sac
of night, and makes me raise
my head: from my window,
I see the killer fire
several times
at the door of my poem,
then disappear in a side street
that leads into my dream;
a boat, on some pier,
awaits him under the stars,
an airplane, a getaway car,
and a thousand feet
come running from the four
corners of the earth,
but no one is being chased.

In the midst of my life,
time and time again,
I see the killer
from my window fire
at the door, then disappear
into a side street
that leads into my days;
the drop of blood on his shoe,
that drop of blood
on his shoe will travel
any distance toward
the next station,
where his victim waits.

I see the killer fire his gun;
the poem crumbles in my hands.

THE MIDWIFE'S HANDS

And, without a covenant,
without a promise of being born,
how shall we live
    with this wind
the hand of sleep
will lay upon the infant's
cradle until the shadows
are dispersed?

The echo knows us,
coming from beyond the world.

The servant of God
knows us, she who lays
a bridge between this world of ours,
and the one beyond.

The wind, the shadow,
the bridge, and the wooden houses
    shaking before the flood.
This birthplace of ours . . .

Life's restless face,
where birth trembles,
and the foetus drops screaming

between the hands
of Umm Youssef,
the midwife.

THIS ROAD ALONE

This road, alone, was left before me.
It is a forest, or rather a tale: dirigibles land on the
roofs as the villagers remove their plague-stricken dead
in wooden carts that rumble away under the cover of
night. While the master shoemaker sleeps fitfully, the
dwarfs get busy mending the shoes.

The desert stretches in my dreams, rife with
promises, with dangers, with cautionary tales.

It is a twofold message, each headed in a different
direction: one vanishes like a squirrel into the
kingdom of flora inside my head, and the other awaits
me like a sentry in front of my door.

And there, in the all-night cafeteria where immigrants
hide their broken teeth in their sleeves when they
laugh, the message like a drop of ink that travels from
iris to iris, lets me know a little secret: the empty glass
on the table that prays

for a few drops of wine, the eyes that stare into the
distance, while Billie Holiday sings from the black core
of her trampled heart: I SLAVED FOR YOU . . .

And the earth floats, a vagabond, among the stars.

A CONVERSATION WITH A PAINTER
IN NEW YORK AFTER THE TOWERS FELL

To Ivan Kustura

"You are the one who will
choose his end at last," my friend
the painter said. "Look at this city.
They buy death cheap, every second,
and sell it to the highest bidder."

He was standing on the edge
of the abyss that hurtles
on the chains of a loft's wide elevator
twelve floors down
to the building's
parking lot.

"She is with us, the bitch.
Call her eternity, or else call her
the clarion of fate.
Everything has its limit;
once you go beyond it,
the storm of mistakes
will start blowing.
It is a casual note
on the page of our present,

that should be carved in stone.

"I see Rodin's finger
in all this. I see him standing
at his 'Gates of Hell',
pointing to a pit from which
the beasts of the future will rise,
where two towers fell
and America lost its head."

THE CORPSE

They tortured the corpse
    until the day broke exhausted,
        and the cock crowed enraged.

They dug their hooks in its flesh.
They beat it with electric cables.
They hung it upside down
from the ceiling fan
for hours on end.

When the torturers grew a bit
    tired, and took a break,
the corpse wiggled its little finger.
It opened its wounded eyes
and muttered something.

Was it asking them for some water?
Was it begging them for a piece of bread?
Was it cursing them, or asking for more?

What did the corpse really want?

THIS MASTER WHO . . .

This is
a master who
came
from America
to drink
from the Tigris
and
the Euphrates.

This is
a thirsty master
who will drink
all the oil
in our wells,
and poison all
the water
in our rivers.

This is
a hungry master
who will devour
our children
by the thousand,
thousands
upon

thousands,
upon thousands.

This is
a master who
has come
to drink blood
from
the Tigris
and the Euphrates.

MASTER

Some leftover
champagne, dead
bubbles fermenting in a glass.
Our party
has come to its end.
Last year
has vanished
in the catacombs of the past,
as if it never were.

On the edge
of the glass, already:
    a fly.

Someone says:
this century is almost
over, perhaps
another master,
less cruel and dumb,
will come
to open a passage
through this wall,
or at least
show us where
the new road begins.

Maybe
we can change.
Tomorrow, we
shall rest.

No, no, no!
the other one says.
Tomorrow,
we shall assassinate
that other, less cruel,
dumb master of yours,
if he ever dares
to come.

WE HEARD THE MAN

This time,
we heard the man
clearly tell the truth:
ap . . . plause . . .
a standing ovation:
at last, the obvious
solution found,
sanctions
lifted at last —
              from now on,
our children
will not starve and die!

Then gradually,
but soon, it was revealed
that this time also
the man had been lying
through his teeth;
one more
disappointment
carefully packaged,
and wrapped
with expensive lies:

        applaaaaaause . . .

this time even louder,
almost deafening – camera
crews, projector lights –
while all around him,
his victims fell
like flies.

A SONG FOR THE ONE WHO
WILL WALK TO THE END OF THE CENTURY

If you happen to stroll
this evening, where
there is no one else,
you will hear the wind
blow savage from the direction
of slaughter, hot like
the breath of a furnace.

It will flap yesterday's
newspaper between your feet,
and make it kiss
the cooling asphalt,
or blindly slap the walls,
then fall dancing
to the floor.

Where you stroll
alone this evening,
the wind will sweep
yesterday's paper away,
and fire will rage inside and out;

it will devour people and buildings,
but never burn down the walls.

WHO KNOWS THE STORY

The century is almost over;
How did it start, when will it end,
against whom is this battle being waged?

Since it began: From the first chapter. Before speech.

Those who stayed behind,
read the writing on the wall.

He who migrated, never found the promised land.

Speak, what will you say?
Or don't speak, and just listen.
Listen to any voice that may reach you.

Toss your old key into the ocean
as long as: no lock, neither a door, nor a house.
Visit our forsaken land sometimes.
The magic ring you covet is to be found there.

The woman you sought after, to no avail,
for so long, awaits you there, now.

Open your hands. Auction off your heart. And hear
   the story.

The day is coming; countless are the signs.
The people ask for bread. The tyrant sees a dream
that defies interpretation.
The peddler of fatwas, purple-clothed
with the blood of sacrifice,
rips through the luxurious fabric of your dreams
with a dagger of righteousness
beating his little tabla all through the night
between your ears – his ultimate joy:
that you never sleep.
The deadlier your migraines, the higher he soars.
It is a world clouded with mysteries.
Mysteries are embedded in words, but
what they tell is only one part of the story.

The audience believed it.
The judge was suspicious of the details.
The scientist thought it was a dance:
between particles and monkeys and trees.
Between the seed, the ant, and Mars
and the galaxies whose giant arms
embrace a cloud of dust.

Don't speak; what will you say?
Or speak, and listen
  to whoever comes along.

The Chinese poet
　dead more than a thousand
years ago, whispers in my ear:
"From this high tower,
I am startled to see
how ferocious is the storm.
The walled city looks empty
when the leaves fall."
　　　　Li Dong

Maybe it's the wind, Master Li Dong,
reciting the story of the flood once more.

My tribe knows it well.
It knows its master and narrator.
It knows its heroes, those windmill shadows
Don Quixote fought valiantly
once upon a time: today
the coughing of a sick child
without medicine behind the walls
of siege, is enough to make it fall.

My tribe. This page. This pen. This wall.
It is the sap, Master. The sap rising
in the trunk of life and the tree.
No. It is the sea of silence, and this
tiny boat has a story.

My friend who died yesterday in exile
battling his final pain,
knew the story from beginning to end
in a single moment of yearning.

Let the current take what it wants.
Let me remain in my place.
Give me this single moment, and let me be:
I want to hear the story.

YOU, THE STORY-TELLER.
THESE: YOUR DAYS.

> *"The storyteller: he is the man who could*
> *let the wick of his life be consumed completely*
> *by the gentle flame of his story."*
>   Walter Benjamin

You tell what you tell,
then crawl in here at last,
into the heart of what you were.

(What you always wanted to be, and are.)

You say what you say;
your sayings end up
as echoes, these echoes
that seem to die.

(Do they end? Or die?)

To those who would
rather listen to what ends,
you speak about
the beginning.
To those who begin
their day at the first page

of the story, you speak
about the end.

It could be a dream.
It could be
the hand of history
writing, erasing, beginning
our yesterdays tomorrow,
inserting our present
into the dying text
of the past.

Maybe this very night
was sliced off from
your own ribs,
to be lived for a while,
to be rendered
into a tale.

But in order
to create your days,
and make them yours,
yours alone,
you need help;
you need compassion,
you need a key, and a door.

You need leaven

for the bread, the light
of childhoods that never end;
the lover, always;
always the guide.

A palm-tree that rises
at the end of your dream.

In order to tell
the story of days
that are yours, yours alone,
you need the rose,
the pain, the pen to fashion
what your days were like,
or tell what you tell,
then crawl at last
in here, into the heart
of what you were
(what you wanted always
to be, and what you became.)

Most likely a dream,
a hand that writes,
or erases, in order for you
to tell about the beginning
to those who would
rather listen to the end.

THE STORY WILL BE TOLD

On the highest deck –
in the lowest dump,
as well – there is always
a story-teller.

The story
     must be told.
Whose story, mine or yours?
Perhaps . . . his, or hers?

No matter from whose
point of view, it will be told:
you, making up a story
          full of gaps about me?
I, narrating your tragi-comical tale?
Perhaps, He, the one
  ignorant of all our days?

It will be told.

Even language itself,
those metaphors hoarded
          like pulp in a giant sponge;
          even the secrets of the tribe
hidden in the moth-eaten

saddlebags of time,
    will find a haven in a slip
from the story-teller's tongue,
a mere stroke of the pen.

So are the tales spun
    from nothing, for a world
that is nothing in the end
but a tale paring its fingernails,
like James Joyce's god,
waiting to be told.

And though it loses
its shine with the passage
of days, yet like a record without
a needle, it shall recite
what details there are: those
worthy of being recited,
to whoever owns
a pair of ears.

IF THE WORDS SHOULD LIVE

The master of selling
    and buying
at the stock exchange,
drops to his knees with a heart attack,
but the war goes on;
the Satanic Mills of money
    never stop turning;
            and with every turn,
                    a siege is laid, a history falls.

You: a poet, sleepless,
            staring at a blank page.

Night around you
might be less of a night,
even death might acquire a sort
of meaning, if these words could live.

For their sake,
    we kill and die,
            and are nourished
by their dazzling poverty.

In words, there is might:

Say *Shaytan*[1],
and the Yazidi[2] will faint with fright.

Say *Allah*, and watch how the fires will burn.

---

1 Shaytan, in Arabic, is the devil
2 The Yazidis are an old oriental religious sect who live in the north
  of Iraq. They worship Tawus Malak who represents the archangel
  Satan, and consider his attitude to be the right one

THE MYSTERY OF WORDS

What the words
can do,
is almost nothing
in these days: a tune
that can barely contain
enough music to make
one dance. Then how are we
to cherish its memory
or sing its praise?
Although
I had seen
more than one
who was shaken as he
listened, and chose
a different way, taking that
road without hesitation, to catch
the mystery
that the words foretell.
I saw you:
It was you who walked
that road, and if it weren't,
then I, alone, was
the one.

THE SKYLIGHT

If you do not open
the skylight, the dove will not
fly into your room.
The water
is ignorant of the reasons
for the latest drought,
the earth is cracked in spite
of the numerous proofs
that testify
to the abundance of water.
Silence is a shell
that will not open itself
if you do not know how
the rose is born, or dies.
A pen on the table,
a notebook that flutters
and unfolds like a Geisha's fan
in the scribe's head;
the poem may get lost
if you don't find the invisible thread.
And the story-teller
may never know
what the story
can tell.

TEA WITH MOUAYED AL-RAWI IN A
TURKISH CAFÉ IN BERLIN
AFTER THE WALL CAME DOWN

Our cigarette packs
close to hand (that secret fuel) . . .
the babble of immigrants
slapping dominoes on marble tops:
a noise once familiar,
out of which a secret word
might flare up like a lit match
amid the smoke, born there,
refusing, here, to die.
If we do not say it, who will?
And who might we be
if we don't?

Not about what came
to pass: how it came, then passed!
But about this spoon buried
in sugar, and this finjan★.
Not that Wall
whose shards are sold
at Checkpoint Charlie
where only yesterday
they exchanged spies,
and traded secrets

of the East and West,
but this Turkish painting
facing us now, with harem
from the days of the Sublime Porte,
who recline dreamily
in pleasure boats,
on a river guzzled down
by history in one gulp!

Let's say we have seen
a lot of walls, how they rise
and fall, how the dust particles
dance under the hooves
of the Mongol's horse,
how "victory" laughs
its idiot's laugh
in the mirror of loss
before it breaks,
and its pieces fill up
the world, where we walk,
and meet, once more.

★   Finjan here is a small tea glass.

ENTRIES FOR A POSSIBLE POEM

Outside
it is suddenly dark.

Above the church tower
night opens its myriad eyes.

The village surrenders
          to the awe
                    of stars.

In the corners
          of the room,
phantoms struggle,
   conquests are many,
defeats numerous.

Stretching his hand,
   he switches on
          the table lamp.

The notebook is open
   on a few sentences,
mostly scratched out.

   Last night's

before-sleep scribbles.

Sketch of a face
            whose owner
he cannot recall.

A woman with a gazelle's
            terrified eyes.

        Storm
    of apprehensions
            flowering into fever.

He picks up the pen
            and, feverish, writes:

This evening,
            this evening –
    no, it is already night.

Back from my usual stroll.

The village
            at this hour:

A fat lady with a small dog
who would always
    greet me

very sweetly
Guten Abend.

Sometimes,
a drunken farmer
dragging his feet
at the end of a festival.

The thin saint
who guards
the ancient steps
of the Gothic church
with a long pole
and pointed hat,
sometimes looks
like my father
in his late illness,
silvered
by the stars.

Did you notice
how many there are?

In my childhood,
we slept on the roofs.

My father taught me
their names.

I live in this village now –
  the stars are almost
      the same.

Somewhere else
      very nearby,
someone is busy
  bombing a sleepy village
identical to this one
      right now.

Many years ago,
      this very one
was bombed also;
      and not very long ago –
         mine.

On a night like this
  sleep is hard to come by.

  I should go out
and see the stars shine
      for one more
         time.

  On a night
like this,

in an age like this,
     wisdom
is a form of despair,
     silence
too often a crime.

Better to cancel
  all tomorrow's
engagements, not
     to answer the phone.

Instead of seeking
     an answer,
find the question.

And for once,
  expose the lie.

Shöppingen, Germany
March / April 1999

A DREAM OF CHILDHOOD

What desire took me
through the seasons
as if by hand . . .

What guides my steps
to that pool hidden
in the country
of childhood: the orchards
aglow with light,
a breeze blowing at noon,
and the red–and–silver
serpent that loved
to wallow in the sun,
lying like a folded
rosary at the bottom
of the pool, under
a face of granite,
by the water
of the lake.

How he started
when I teased him
with a ruler,
probed him gently
with a pencil,

or dropped a small
pebble on his back.
He thrashed wildly
and spun off,
as if stung by a bolt,
causing the sun
to be banished from the pool,
as the water turned
murky with sediment,
that drifted slowly
in his wake.

And I remember
a hawk in flight,
clutching a fish
between his claws,
still twisting
to break free.

A BOY AGAINST THE WALL

Leaning against the wall
near the blackened brick oven,
the boy waves a blueberry branch
before his face, and buries
his eyes in its leaves,
too ashamed to endure
their stares, those neighbours
leaning over the walls
like a gathering of crows,
policemen's badges flashing
in the sun, and his father,
still in his pyjamas,
flogged with a belt
in the middle of the yard.

BUTTERFLY DREAM

The butterfly
that fluttered as if tied
with an invisible thread
to paradise, almost
brushed my chin
as I sat on my favourite
bench in the garden,
shaking last night's
nightmares
from my head,
and drank my coffee
in the sun.
How beautiful it was,
as it glided over
the fence,
like a tiny prayer or dream,
that only yesterday
was a mere caterpillar,
trapped in its narrow cocoon.

THE FACE

On the bridge
that spans the white
Montmartre cemetery
buried with all its dead
beneath the snow,
that face
as it went by –
a woman walking
aimless, oblivious
of the wind
that lifted her skirt
above her thighs,
of pedestrians and cars,
who wept bitterly
and bit her nails,
from that moment on
has been haunting
your eyes:
whenever you cross
a bridge, you can
almost see it
going by.

WITNESSES ON THE SHORE

In the beginning,
we heard the roaring . . .

In the beginning,
before we could see,
when mountains' knees
knocked together,
and the world's
hidden dam collapsed:
it came roaring,
carrying
unhinged doors,
trees with all their roots,
storks' nests and coffins,
carriages and horses.
It carried a sentry-box
still festooned with a flag,
a bride's dresser
with its three
shimmering mirrors
before we saw the cradle
carried along by the waves,
the woman swimming
close behind it, her burning
eyes, her floating braid.

Who will stop the world
from being swept away,
or close the gates
of doom for our sake?
With what stone?

No one.

Who will bring back
the figure that has departed,
who will lift the child
from its cradle
like a bird
from between the claws
of the dragon, and let
the mother reach him,
even as she drowns?

No one.

Only a single man
who flung himself cursing
into the current,
whom the raging river
received like a libation,
struggled for a while,
shouted once, then
was seen no more.

This is what we saw
on the morning of the flood,
we the witnesses on the shore.

NOTES FROM A TRAVELLER

When I saw
death make its
ablutions
in the public fountain,
and people drift
in their sleep
along the roads,
all my dreams
seemed to be
nothing but pyramids
of sand
that crumbled
before my eyes.

The light
of my days fled
in the opposite
direction, away
from that city
of the damned.

Free to choose
how to begin
our journey,
we are

chosen at last,
and there is
no other way
but the way.

DIMENSIONS

The oud player
in his darkened corner
hugs his instrument ever so gently
as if listening to the foetus kick
inside the belly of a pregnant woman,
while his fingers torture
the strings.

The belly-dancer's body
under the burning lights is truly
possessed, writhing in the fourth
dimension of ecstasy, where
tickets are seldom sold.

We, the spectators, stay here
with the chairs, facing
an empty stage.

WITNESS

With a sensitive ear
and unseeing eye,
the blind man advanced,
his white stick like a woodpecker
tapping its way along the street,
over the sticky asphalt,
where the massacre took place,
the victims long since
removed, the ambulances
with wailing sirens
vanished into the distance.

WIDOW MAKER, MOTHER OF WOES

(From an Iraqi Poet)

You,
widow maker,
you, mother of woes;

We know
your heart is a stone.

We know
what is written
in your great book
of stone:

for us,
always the mourning,
for you always
the victory
parade.

THE SCORPION IN THE ORCHARD

Black are the hostile forms
in the patches of mud, amidst the kingdoms
of dry moss, after the noon cools off
and the shadow lingers
like a dark history
in between the vines
hanging over the wall:
the garden loses its heat
like a jewel the lady of the house
takes off at the end of the party
and lays in its box
lined with black velvet.
The crackling of dry sticks,
a thread of ash dispersed
as if by the blowing from
the mouth of a toothless god,
and suddenly night is
as it never was: the scorpion's stinger is high
and curved while it advances
like a bulldozer
on the path,
in order to mix cement
with blood on a certain summer's night,
to crucify the foot
on the block of belligerent time

at the entrance to hell, at the gate
of a lost paradise . . .
I convulse, leaping out of my trance,
barefoot in the orchard,
and throw at that bulldozer sailing through the air
anything within my reach,
my finjan, my pen, my book,
a twitch, a spell, a hoarse cry,
a curse, my shoe.

THE EXECUTIONER'S FEAST

When
the executioner
pitched his tent
in the middle
of our garden, and set
his wine and cup
upon the grass
to celebrate
victory at the end
of massacre, we saw
the flowers flutter shut
like the eyes
of the dying
and the stars
go blind.

WAR CHILD

*To an Iraqi child who was born
in war, and died in war*

The child came back,
she who was lost at war.

She stands at the end
of the corridor
a candle in her hand.

I see her when I wake
in the first hour
of dawn, as if she
awaited my certain clash
with the real,
her eyes large
and full of
patience.

Wizened beyond
her years, she stands
in the waste-land
where my thoughts get lost,
where my voice

falters, which could have
disturbed the assassin
with a few simple
questions, the answers to which
she somehow seems
to know.

How long will it
last, this war, child?
How many more nights
at the bottom of this
bottomless well?
What would the four-star general do
if they were to deprive his own child
of milk and bread?

She says: they have
taken my folks in a ship
to the other world,
and left me here
with you.

Sargon Boulus

HULAGU THE HUN'S EXULTATION★

(2nd Series)

My horses
are swifter
than the wind.

Their hooves
throw off sparks
as we enter
the darkened
cities.

Eager as a bride
in her tent
of flames,
war awaits me,
and destiny speaks
in my name.

For I am Hulagu:
a sword restless
in its scabbard,
whose shadow
breeds a cloud

of vultures
wherever
it falls.

Refugees
see me coming
in their nightmares
among the ruins,

and captives beg
for a handful of hay
from my horse.

---

* Hulagu (c.1217-1265), a grandson of Genghis Khan, is best known
for having sacked Baghdad, in January, 1258.

Sargon Boulus

KNIFE SHARPENER

An opening
laced with splinters
of glass, where
creation bodies forth
its myriad forms:
everyone comes
to enter this alley –
it is a world.

Dervishes
who lie in caves
with scorpions and snakes,
dogs that chase cars
in a wedding procession.

He who was
due to come, the one
destined to leave,
the accused,
the witness,
and judge.

This world
is a carter who groans
under the weight

of the flour sack,
it is the peddler
of bitter salt,
the rabab player
who begs from
door to door.

This opening
in my memory
where I trace
a shadow that takes me
across the seasons,
and listen
to a half-buried tune
that echoes
in a remote chamber
of my mind . . .

This eternity
that swims in my head,
this crow
that comes to tarnish
its whiteness.

Crawling from
house to house,
he comes
at the peak of noon –

no one but a boy
playing in the shade,
and a woman
bringing grass
to the lamb tethered
to a stake –
he comes,
for the world
is choking with rust,
and those who sleep
indoors, dream
who knows
of what feast,
on the day
when they break
their fast.

He appears
at the entrance
of the alley, his face
bony and grim,
a blind man's
goggles covering
his eyes,
the contraption
of leather and flint-stone
strapped to his back;
a man, almost,

a scarecrow, a freak
hungry for
the taste of iron,
regurgitated by the sun.

The knife
sharpener appears
like a forgotten omen
in the kingdom
of rusting things,
and grinds his stone
to make the sparks fly
between his hands,
croaking
to the sleepers
that he has come,
come to sharpen
their knives.

THE SAINT'S MOUNTAIN

The sky
is a Persian
carpet with brilliant
patterns, rolled
by an invisible hand,
over the hump
of San Bruno
mountain★.

I see it from
my eastern window,
a whale of dust,
whose pink ravines brim
with shadows
at dusk,
until the fog
shrouds it in its veils.

Once, I went
and climbed it,
and stood
at the summit,
where the radio
towers are.

Knife Sharpener

Today, I pace
through the house,
and when I pass
by the window,
I steal a look
at the mountain,
where the lights
flash red
on the towers,
and stab the sky.

EXECUTION OF THE FALCON

A gambler I met
at a gas station
near Reno
in the Nevada desert
(bearded, his eyes
two emeralds plucked
from the devil's own garden,
shaded by a ten-gallon hat,
his hand buried
in a huge glove with
a metal ring),
told me that he spent
years and years training
his falcon to hunt,
but now it has lost its
"killer instinct", he said –
as if talking
about an old boxer –
and now it's not much more
than a chicken.

"Now watch, son," he said
as he showed me his bird,
shabby-feathered,
drugged with hunger

or sleep, then he let it loose
from the ring to fly.
And with his other
naked hand, he picked up
his rifle, and aimed
with one eye.

Before the falcon
could begin to soar,
it dropped off
and hit the ground;
its right wing
stirred for a last time,
and raised
a tiny plume of dust.

It was a bundle of feathers
the man picked up
almost tenderly,
and ruffled the broken wing
with his fingers.
Then he tossed it
onto the flatbed of his
pick-up, and roared off
into the desert
and the night.

A FEW MOMENTS IN THE GARDEN

A few evenings
at the back of the house,
under the weak sun,
dry ferns barely blocking
from my sight
the glittering shards of glass
stuck on top of the fence.
I sit here to count
the seconds,
to understand
what it means to leave,
or stay in my place,
dreaming without
the need to pursue my dream,
silent when I wish
I could scream.
In front of my neighbours'
houses, big flags flutter
in the wind.
America's generals
are preparing the engines
of ruin; the drums of war
are beaten, and night deepens.
Neither this glimpse
I glean from nature's epic

can lead me to the dark
secret of its solace
one day,
nor will that road-bend
in my memory
allow me to see the mask
that flees always before me
into the alleys
of my life.

The truth is, I'm here,
in this corner; my hands
folded in my lap, my eye
follows a mosquito
that drones among the leaves
of grass, flies over the fence,
and takes my thoughts
into the unknown
for a moment,
during which I don't
even think, neither dream
nor desire anything.
A moment worthy
of a true Buddhist monk.
Then those evenings
were gone, and I was back
in the world of the mad.

THE APACHES

They say, the Apaches –
who were exterminated
to a last man, and nothing
survives but their name,
which is given
to a deadly helicopter –
after they had fasted
for long, and hunger
had drained their strength,
when they heard the earth
rumble under their feet,
and knew that the buffaloes
had come, mounted their horses
without saddles, and rushed
eagerly toward the herd.

Hardly a single warrior
had enough strength left
in his arm to draw his bow,
yet somehow one managed
to draw it to his breast,
and shot the buffalo in the heart.

For the Apaches knew
the Great Spirit when it called

and invited them to battle.

Likewise the poet,
who is besieged by the cries
of his tribe as he wanders
among the bones
and walks through the ruins
of his city; he dreams
of flying like an eagle
over the heads of the slain
and their slayers,
hoping to catch a fabulous
creature swift in its flight
with his words,
and to plant the hook
of his imagination
into the flesh of his prey.

Sargon Boulus

THE LETTER ARRIVED

You said
that you write while the bombs
rain down, erase the history of the roofs,
eradicate the faces of the houses.

You said:
I write to you while God
allows them to write my destiny;
this is what makes me doubt He is God.

You wrote to say:
My words, these creatures threatened
with fire. Without them, I wouldn't be able to live.

After "they" are gone, I will regain them
with all their purity like my white bed
in the barbarians' dark night.

I keep vigil in my poem until dawn, every night.

Then you said:
I need a mountain, a sanctuary. I need other humans.

And you sent the letter.

THE MAN FELL

In the middle of the square
      the man fell to his knees.

– Was he so tired
that he could no longer stand on his feet?

– Did he reach that wall
where the spent wave of our life breaks?

– Could it be that sorrow
knocked him down with its invisible hammer?

Was it the whirlwind of pain?

– Maybe it was a tragedy nobody can endure.

– Maybe it was the angel of mercy
      who came with his feathery axe
            when he was due to come.

– Maybe it was God or the devil.

In the middle of the square
the man fell suddenly like a horse
whose knees were harvested with a scythe.

LEGACY WITH A TASTE OF DUST

These books that are closed
        to the world:
our sufferings, with a taste of dust.

This legacy; a heaven betrayed by the eye.

A god who forgot his heavy boot
        forever upon our necks.

He plays his black requiem
        on the harpsichord of our bones
at the court of king night.

With every tune, a head rolls.

And one day the land is a wasteland.

One day only the barbed wire
        laid by the conquerors remains.

The wind alone comes down
to bleed like a mother, and scream
        and give birth.

– But, who was here before us, before

we came?

– Why, there was the house, and those
who lived in the house?

And this wind?

HE WHO COMES

From far away, he comes:
no one knows when, or where.

After a time in which
we patiently wait, in which we eat
the bitter bread of wisdom.
It might be a sleepless night.
It might be an age that
passes in the twinkling of an eye.

Between the traveller's step
and the arrow that points the way
in stone. Between the chirring crickets
and the silence of the fields
ravaged by the latest storm –
a worm drops from Enkidu's nose:
Gilgamesh is no longer king.
There is no Uruk.
Nothing is left
but the wolf's pelt
and wilderness, where he shall wander and mourn.

He comes from far away:
no one knows when, or where.

THE POUCH OF DUST

The woman they called
Umm Mohammed, the fortune-
teller around whose skinny neck
hangs what looks like a necklace
but is only a black leather pouch
she said contains a handful
of dust from home . . .
the one who squats on
a wooden crate in Hashimiyya square
in Amman, with a thousand others
like her, who wait for a visa
that will take them anywhere,
she who knew
as she crossed the border
she might never see home again,
and now shall carry this black pouch
of dust like a yoke around
her neck wherever
she goes.

Sargon Boulus

THE ZIGGURAT BUILDERS

They were
the first dreamers
who embodied the shape
of a dream in clay:
a stairwell of prayers
that will scale
the heights.

They knew:
a stranger once
passed among them,
and disappeared.
His shade
will be redeemed
in the form
of a ziggurat –
this ship of the gods
whose figurehead
will rend the clouds.

And learned:
it is a sea of time,
on whose shore
from time to time,
we might glimpse

an ancestor's
figure in white,
who will nod to us

across a thousand years
and wait for his ship.

Sargon Boulus

THE LEGEND OF AL-SAYYAB AND THE SILT

From the start, Al-Sayyab[1] knew
that the things we love
  are few: a face
shining under the rags
  in its tiny cradle
luminous like a loaf of bread.
Several women, kind
  like the nursemaids of legend
and a handful of silt
moist like a chronicle of the flood –
These kept pursuing him
  out of the apertures
      of his memory,
the windows he saw in childhood
      opening for his gaze.

For these, he sang
  even as he burned
      and waited on hospital beds
away from the water of Iraq.
      For these.
He begged even the mud at the
        bottom of a stream.
    And sang.

Al-Sayyab knew from the start:
a barefoot will lead only
to jail or massacre, and poverty
                              is the only devil
as long as the world in its splendour
or misery, is a banquet thrown
                        for the others
    in our name . . .
And whenever he wrote the poem,
the hospital plunged like a raft
    down into the void.

Then, as night, that solicitous
servant, brought him
the halo of eternity, and death like a faceless
dancer in the earth's last tavern
disrobed for his eyes –
            Jaikur[2] turned
with all its orchards
    and all its mud
            in the river of his blood
and he saw the Lord
at the bottom of Buwaib[3].

---

1 Badr Shaker Al-Sayyab (1926-1964) was a pioneering Iraqi poet who
   spent the last years of his life in hospitals, in Beirut, London, Kuwait.
2 Jaikur is the town where Al-Sayyab was born
3 Buwaib is the river that runs through Jaikur

O PLAYER IN THE SHADOWS

I play alone.   An hour.   Or two.
I spread the cards on the table.

When will you show up?
Player, all this luck is for you.
Appear. I will stay up until dawn
   waiting for your sight.
To whom will I show my cards?
Without you, what meaning to my game?
I will play. But first,
   what are the rules: if I'm to win,
who might the loser be?
   if I'm the loser, who will win
                        . . . what?

O player in the shadows,
this game will not reveal its secrets
   without a price: a thousand
dinars for the one who will show his hand.
Another thousand for him
         who shall keep it concealed.

Strange. What a game!
   in which no one can win, or lose.
Yes. And what a jackpot. What stakes!

A KEY TO THE HOUSE

A man dreamt
   that he left
his city, one day, in a storm
that was bending the fields;
columns of dust rose at its approach
on the outskirts of a hamlet
that rode the wind, and wove
around his feet.

A man dreamt
   that a woman
with a child in her arms
sang a song he knew
from childhood
and kept repeating to himself
as he crossed the desert
as if it were
his only well.

But a voice warned him
in the midst of his dream.
A darkness fell
         suddenly on the plain.

A bird soared out of a tree

whose abandoned bough
kept tipping at air –
      silence deepened
until he could hear time
sneak past a dying orchard
light-footed as a fox or a quail.

Water shook and splintered
as he bent, in his thirst, to drink
and the river
  swept his reflection away
in its widening circles
while he tried to salvage
      what was left
with his cupped hand, in a hurry now
for the sun
  had begun to sink
      like a magical windowpane
across the border
that he envisioned for so long.
And was crossing now.

Before anyone could call
his name, he turned and looked.
He left his suitcase
in the middle of the road.
From his hand that shuddered
  – slit by the only thing it held: the key

to his father's house –
hot drops of blood dribbled,
      and fell in the dust.

This is the line –
  here your first path
      comes to an end.
Rub the dust out of your eyes,
and look: this land of the others,
      where you shall tread.

NEWS ABOUT NO ONE

Those who are
   never in the news,
whom no one remembers –
what wind erased their traces
as if they never walked the earth;
my father, all the others, where
    O where . . . ?

What happened to the
   neighbourhood carpenter
maker of solid beds, and dressers
     for brides?
How he worshipped the wood!

Where is the silent shoemaker
who hugged his anvil, and bit the bitter nails
between his teeth? Did a "smart" bomb
demolish his hole-in-the-wall
crammed to the ceiling
with battered shoes?

Where the coppersmith,
   where the golden tray?

The ear of wheat around the saint's image?

The horseshoe above the door?
What happened to Umm Youssef, the midwife?
How many babies were dragged
   out of the warm darkness of the womb
into the starkness of this world
   by her dexterous hands
sending them on their way
   with a slap on their bare bottoms
through the crooked valleys of
            their destinies, soldiers who fight
            in dubious battles
            and unjust wars? . . .

After they got tired
slaving in the mills of poverty
to fill the granaries of the tyrant
did they feel ashamed of the way
                this world is made?

After the sieges, after the wars
beyond hunger, beyond
            enemies, out of the reach
of the executioner's hand –
            did they go to sleep
   at last?
To sleep, and hug the dust.

REMARKS TO SINDBAD FROM THE OLD MAN OF THE SEA

Our quest
has barely begun.
and you are already tired!
Forget the sea.
Stop dreaming of the ships . . .
For you there's no more
trading to be done.
I'm the last
voyage you'll ever make
and was your first one as well.

Every way
you came by, every road
you took, I paved with my own hands
for your sake.
And you still complain!
Too heavy on your
shoulders, dear Sindbad?
That's because
I carry on my back
eternity's weight plus my own
and need your legs to take me around
in my travels between
night and day.

You will try
to escape, time after
time, I know: dream that you crush
my head with a heavy stone
every night, and dance
drunkenly over
my corpse.

But if you happen
to venture into that jungle
on your own, night around you
will only deepen; hear a serpent
hiss in every whisper, see a foe
in the friend's eye.
And in short,
trap and poison shall become
your lot everywhere
you go.

Don't try to escape
and forget the sea.
Stop dreaming of the ships . . .
For you, there's no more
trading to be done.
Today you have unbound
the knot of my waiting and
from now on, Sindbad, you will

carry me on your
powerful back,
to explore
  this island
      together:
I and thou, you and I, as one.

INVOCATIONS BEFORE SAILING

Be with him if you will
the sleepless one on his night journey

Visit his unfurnished cave
by the distant shore of the poem:

Go to the water source
and come back dying of thirst.

You would be foolish
to put your heart in chains

One day you may need every one
of its countless mistakes:

Armed with a simple bow
and some arrows, let it go . . .

If it must hunt the unicorn,
first it has to enter the forest.

Let there be always under your feet
some generous land to make you feel safe.

If one day it proves to be
too narrow, find the sea. And sail.

Saadi Youssef and Sargon Boulus

Khalida Said, Margaret Obank, Adonis and Sargon Boulus

Fadhil al-Azzawi, Abbas Beydoun and Sargon Boulus

Amjad Nasser, Sargon Boulus and Saif al-Rahbi

Sargon Boulus in an interview with Margaret Obank

Sargon Boulus and Etel Adnan in her home in Paris

Joachim Sartorious, Sargon Boulus and Hans Magnus Enzensberger in Yemen, 2002

Sargon Boulus and his friend and publisher, Iraqi poet Khalid al-Maaly

Sargon Boulus with Allen Ginsberg in San Francisco

Charles Boyle reading with Sargon Boulus, Poetry Café, London, 1998

Sargon Boulus and Mouayed al-Rawi at the Berlin Wall

Sargon Boulus and Khaled Mattawa

Sargon Boulus facing the head of Seamus Heaney, Dublin Writers' Centre

Samuel Shimon and Sargon Boulus on O'Connell Bridge, Dublin

Tributes

to

SARGON BOULUS

from
fellow poets and authors in the Arab world

The death of the Iraqi poet Sargon Boulus (1944–2007) left a gaping wound in the heart of modern Arabic poetry. Arab cultural pages and websites overflowed with reminiscences of Sargon's monumental presence through his unique poetry, and great sorrow over his untimely departure.

The following are excerpts from the hundreds of articles celebrating his life and mourning his departure.

Sinan Antoon
New York, October 2007

THE ONLY IRAQI POET
Saadi Youssef

Sargon Boulus is the only Iraqi poet. This might sound confusing, but it is clear to me. Sargon Boulus entered poetry through its narrow door. He started in the early 1960's, fully equipped and with his craftsmanship fully formed. Surprising and yet wise at the same time (he did not have that waywardness which is necessary at times for a poet who is about to storm the field). Sargon Boulus did not storm the field. He entered it calmly and lovingly. He was not competitive, but used to give advice and represent the mature poetic culture as opposed to enmity, conflict, and false pretence. He never bragged about his knowledge, even though he had every right to do so. He considered poetry the product of both a deep culture and a tangible experience. Sargon Boulus hates pretence. . . I say he is the only poet.

He was not political in any way, but he was far more courageous than many of the poets who used politics to lift them when it could, but who abandoned it when it involved danger.

He was against the occupation of Iraq, not as a politician, for Sargon Boulus was never a politician. He stood against occupation because the poet must be against occupation. His stance was sublime, because his poem is sublime . . . I hardly know any prose poem

practitioner who knew its complexities and responsi-
bilities the way Boulus did . . .

★ ★ ★

THE SARGONIAN POEM
Elias Khoury

Before his death, Sargon Boulus threw *Another Bone for
the Tribe's Dog* in the form of a collection of poems to
appear soon from al-Jamal publishing house. However,
this bone will not lead us to the place he named Where
City in his first collection *Arrival in Where City*, because
that ambiguous city will remain the poet's secret, one
he will only divulge in the form of a poem. And we
will have to reconstitute the city from the shards of the
Sargonian poem, which will only make the matter
more ambiguous . . .

When I read Sargon's poetry and that of the second
generation of Arab modernist poets I am struck with
fear. The first founding generation guarded itself from
the poetic unknown by developing the old poetic val-
ues and/or leaning on the western modernist tradition.
As for this generation, it launched its experience with-
out protection or reference. It is true it was influenced
by various international experiences, but that did not
protect it, nor did it form a stable reference. It is the

generation of human and linguistic rootlessness. The generation of exiles and writing on non-existent walls. And that is why its experience seems akin to linguistic shards. It is the daughter of total nudity, which covers itself with words only to find itself more nude and dis-illusioned.

It is not easy to be an Assyrian, an Iraqi, and an immigrant without a supporting reference. Sargon was all of these and he was a poet. . . I don't want to ele-gize. We must accustom ourselves not do so. A poet's death is not the most important event in his life. All people die. The poem is the event and it is an event that is renewed with each reading.

★ ★ ★

IRAQIS ARE EPIC PEOPLE
Ounsi el-Hage

Iraqis are epic people, even when they sing of the sin-gular self. Sargon Boulus, who was extinguished a few days ago in Berlin, was a representative of the mytho-logical power of the land of Nimrud, water, and Gil-gamesh . . .

Boulus escaped Iraq and went to Lebanon and from Lebanon he flew to California. From California he would sing wherever he happened to be until he perched on a hospital in Germany. The wandering Assyrian. Not anyone can be an Assyrian. Not every-one can be a poet, or an Iraqi, or a wanderer. Not everyone, not even anyone, except someone who can write this line: "to drag death with him". Or, more correctly: to drag life behind him.

★ ★ ★

THE ASSYRIAN'S BOAT
Amjad Nasser

We will not meet again, because you will not come to London where my tattered sails threw me after a long journey, just like yours, in search of Treasure Island. Perhaps your body, that tired boat, will be pushed one day by smugglers beyond the borders; perhaps it will stay in Berlin. Or your Assyrian family who were exiled from Mesopotamia to America might request it. That is not important. It is not important where the body goes, as long as the boat has docked, at last, where all boats do.

But surely the soul (if it be anything but this eager tiger behind the ribcage) will go to its first place. To those dusty streets and wild sun and blatant clarity of things. There in al-Habbaniyah or Kirkuk where those mysterious builders of boats and sails were busy readying the Assyrian's boat for travel. I am almost certain. Perhaps because you were one of the most Iraqi of all the Iraqis I have known. Perhaps because you are a poet and the poet, for some reason, always returns to the there.

★ ★ ★

THE VAGABOND POET
Abdo Wazen

Every collection he published was a poetic surprise. Although prolific in writing, he rarely published. He preferred to stay away from the limelight. The poem, in his view, is a moment in life as it is a moment etched in the heart of language. Poetry was a lived experience as well as an experience of writing, contemplation, vision, and encounter . . .

His immense knowledge, especially in world poetry, established his uniqueness as a poet and his pioneering nature, for he founded a new kind of poem and an atmosphere that did not exist before him. He may appear to be rootless or without any ancestors in the poetic sense, but he was able to establish and found his own poetics on the exilic condition and rootlessness, despite his strong relation to Arabic poetry, both classical and modern . . . He had a great impact on subsequent generations. Young poets were eager to read and emulate him. They found in him the father who refused to practise his patriarchy and a poet who always renewed himself in his rebellion against rhetoric, his openness to the ephemeral and quotidian, and in being seduced by imagination and the unconscious.

The vagabond poet is tired of travel. The cities he confronted have drained him, but he did not return to his city like Odysseus. He died, as he lived, a stranger, exiled in the heart of the world.

★ ★ ★

HIS OVERWHELMING LEGACY
Abbas Beydhoun

I consider Sargon Boulus to be the closest to me out of all of the contemporary Arab poets. As soon I read his poems in *Mawaqif* [in 1969] I was amazed. That was one of those moments when we feel the spark of poetry penetrating us. It was, to be sure, a discovery. Sargon never ceased to surprise us . . . He was one of our most mature and experienced poets and one who was the closest to the ideal poet. But Sargon, who was struck by poetry in his life as well as in his writing, was led by poetry on life's paths into distant areas where we could not follow him.

Thus we found him many times abandoning the market of poetry and that of publishing and criticism. And now that he has left us so prematurely, not in years, but in terms of his potential, we know that we have to search more and more to meet this man. Sargon Boulus has left a great deal for us to read in our coming days. Now that he is gone, we can longer pass by with our usual laziness before his overwhelming legacy.

★ ★ ★

TO SARGON, POETRY WAS SOMETHING AKIN TO MAGIC
Fadhil al-Azzawi

I knew Sargon as a genuine poet from the first moment I met him in Kirkuk in 1958 when we were still students . . . Perhaps Sargon was the only person in the world with whom poetry was the only subject we discussed, as if the world was only created for poetry. Everything else was secondary and of no important value. Every time we met we used to read our poems and discuss the most important works we had just discovered, the ones by American and British poets and writers whose works we used to follow with the full force of literature which alone gave meaning to our lives. Forty years later we were both invited to a poetry festival in Sana'a, Yemen, and Sargon said to me: Did you see? When we used to sit in Atlas café in Kirkuk we never thought poetry could ever lead us to Sana'a, but it has. Isn't there something akin to magic in this?

Yes, to him, poetry was something akin to magic. Every sentence and every word was a creation of the world anew; therefore one must always be careful when inventing one's chemical and poetic formula, for any mistake could be lethal.

Sargon did not like employment and dedicated his life to poetry. He believed that poetry and work don't go together. If you want to be a poet you must give your entire life to poetry and even more than life if you can. But that has its exorbitant price in accepting the solitude you impose on yourself.

In the long period Sargon spent in San Francisco he always suffered loneliness and solitude, both of which affected his spirits and the vitality of his body. He used to avail himself of any opportunity to escape his American prison to be among his many friends and loved ones. It was, of course, a risk on his part, having just survived heart problems, to leave America for a few months to attend a poetry festival in Lodève and another in Rotterdam, then to move to Berlin, ignoring his body's pains and doctors' advice. But, in doing so, with his poetic imagination, he was escaping a more lethal beast, that of his solitude. Sargon never thought that he could die – and he was right.

★ ★ ★

AN IMMENSE FREEDOM
Kadhim Jihad Hassan

With Sargon, Arabic poetry witnessed a rare condition; that of a poet who dedicated his entire life, thought, and human powers to poetry alone. Sargon did not wish to be part of a settled or fixed life whose features were defined and whose tasks were known. He accepted impoverishment and suffered the neglect of Arab and other cultural institutions, because he cherished this immense freedom, which for him formed the essential counterpart for poetry and its only ally. An immense freedom coupled with immense work on poetry and a constant work on language itself.

I do not know an Arab poet who celebrated this continuous work on language as Sargon did, or someone who was more consumed by amending his writings. He would not give one page for publication unless he was sure that it was right and that it followed a winged motion here, and was intentionally slow there, as he wished it to be. Sargon was knowledgeable in world poetry in its highest forms. He encountered them through their best translations into English and he frequented Arabic poetry, especially the classical tradition. Abu Tammam, whom Sargon considered his master, side by side with Rilke, would get the lion's share of Sargon's admiration. But it wasn't the ambiguous or pedantic Abu Tammam, but Abu Tammam the craftsman in the dynamic and original sense of the word. The man of constant and hard work and the worker who is always bent and holding his hammer. He who works on the poem even as he walks, sleeps, or dreams.

★ ★ ★

HE SHINES IN HIS POEMS
Khalid al-Maaly

An essential poet and perhaps the most important contemporary poet after al-Sayyab? You read him in many languages and he shines in his poems. His language is lucid and his thought knit with such care rarely to be found in the dominant poetry in the Arab world these days.

AFTERWORD

"It just grabbed me, this magic of words, of music"

Sargon Boulus passed away on Monday morning, 22 October 2007, in hospital in Berlin. Many of his friends knew that he had been very ill, but in the summer of 2007 he had recovered enough to come to Europe and read his poems at poetry festivals in Lodève and Rotterdam.

It is so difficult to accept that Sargon will not be writing any more poems, will not be at the end of a telephone, or coming to visit. He will not be sloping off to lie on his bed with a book of poetry and a glass of red wine. He died too soon, only 63. He had been writing poetry since he was 12 years old, and having his work published a couple of years later; in his own words "since then, I haven't stopped".

Born into an Assyrian Iraqi family in Al-Habbaniyah, he grew up near the well-known Lake Habbaniyah, built by the British for the military camp where his father worked. The young Sargon would sneak glimpses of the "English ladies in summertime among their flowers and lawns . . . a vision of paradise" when he visited the camp with his father. He was the only writer in his family, although his brother built up a good library, and he never forgot the intense and rich background that he came from.

He felt that in some way he was "chosen" to see the world through words. Not only was he "chosen" but he was held tightly in the thrall of words. "The Arabic language really has that magic and once it reveals itself to you, you are trapped," he told me when I interviewed him at length for the first issue of *Banipal*. His profound sensitivity to language – and above all to Arabic – to its essential development as part of human history and experience, and particularly its expression in poetry, changed his life and drew him almost exclusively to books and writing.

When he first discovered English, borrowing his brother's books, and with fellow poet Jean Dammo (1942-2003) buying up second-hand books on Baghdad market stalls, he read "like a madman". He immersed himself in poetry, all day and every day, reading it, writing it, translating it, thinking it, discussing it and performing it.

When you got him talking about poets and poetry, he opened up like a rose, suddenly, colourfully, in continuous bloom. It is no wonder that young Arab poets, and particularly women poets, flocked to his readings in the Arab world. In spite of his nearly 40 years in San Francisco, he never stopped writing in Arabic or being thrilled by its power and richness. He became one of the best-known and popular contemporary Arab poets.

Sargon never sought celebrity or prizes, he published his work sparingly in Arabic and hardly at all in translation – mainly in the pages of *Banipal*, for which he was a long-standing editor and prodigious poetry translator. We had planned to make amends and were working closely with him on this selection of his poems in translation, *Knife Sharpener*, when he died, his body unable any more to accept the rejection it had long suffered. The volume is now transformed into a commemoration and celebration of Sargon's still much-needed voice. Sargon Boulus lived – and lives still – in his poetry.

Margaret Obank
London, 2009

ACKNOWLEDGEMENTS

"Notes for a Traveller" was published in *The Wolf*, Number 19, December 2008

Earlier versions of some translations were published in Banipal magazine:

Banipal 18, Autumn 2003 – "The Skylight", "A Boy Against the Wall", "Butterfly Dream", "The Executioner's Feast", "Execution of the Falcon", "The Apaches" and "The Pouch of Dust".

Banipal 12, Autumn 2001 – "The Story will be Told", "Tea with Mouayed al-Rawi in a Turkish Café in Berlin after the Wall came down", "A Dream of Childhood", "The Ziggurat Builders", "The Legend of Al-Sayyab and the Silt", "O Player in the Shadows", "A Key to the House" and "News about No one".

Banipal 8, Summer 2000 – "This Road Alone", "The Corpse", "A Song for the One who will Walk to the End of the Century", "The Face", "Hulagu the Hun's Exultation", "Remarks to Sindbad from the Old Man of the Sea".

Banipal 5, Summer 1999 – "Entries for a Possible Poem".

Banipal 4, Spring 1999 – "Who Knows the Story".

Banipal 1, February 1998, "Master", "We Heard the Man", "If the Words should Live", "Dimensions" and "Invocations Before Sailing".

The poems were translated by Sargon Boulus from several of his Arabic collections, among them *Hamil al-Fanous fi Lail el-Dhi'ab* (1996), *Idha Kunta Na'iman fi Markabi Nooh* (1998), and *Al-Awal wa'l-Tali* (2000), and from unpublished works.

The Foreword by Adonis and all the Tributes were from the Arabic translated by Sinan Antoon.